THE BULLET TAKES FOREVER

THE BULLET TAKES FOREVER

Heidi Kasa

Mouthfeel Press is an indie press. We publish poetry, fiction, and nonfiction in English and Spanish by new and established poets and writers.

Cover Design: Enzo Rodríquez Suárez
Interior Design: Kimberly James

Contact Information: info.mouthfeelbooks@gmail.com

ISBN: 978-1-957840-42-0
Library of Congress Control Number: 2025945417

Published in the United States, 2025

First Printing in English
$18

CONTENTS

To all those who've been affected by gun violence.

In honor of Mrs. Ara Duke, whose brilliance lives on in us.

PREFACE

It's no secret that America is having a cultural crisis around guns. There's an epidemic of gun violence and polarized beliefs—and conspiracy theories—about mass shootings. From 2020 to 2022, firearms killed more children and teens than any other cause. Not only mass or school shootings—this is the daily environment of many children.

I don't pretend to be objective on the issue of gun violence. I'm a parent of two young children, one of whom experienced a lockdown at her kindergarten in 2021 and several active shooter drills. In 2022, one year after moving to Texas, I experienced an active shooter situation. One month later, the school shooting in Uvalde occurred. In 2024, during the period when most of this book had already been written, my daughter's kindergarten teacher was killed as a bystander at a shooting during a concert.

I wrote these poems because I needed to, not because I wanted to. I can't look away from how these events have affected me. The poems chronicle my experiences, bear witness to my feelings, and explore a larger range of psychological fractures and healing.

I am affected by these shootings. You are affected by these shootings— regardless of parenting status. This is important to acknowledge.

We are in a constant state of trauma in America when we just have to wait another day for another shooting, besides the millions of Americans who live with guns as a daily reality. We need to look at this. The normalization of this violence is unacceptable.

One politician said: "It's an unspeakable tragedy." I agree it's a tragedy. I wonder, if we speak about this tragedy, can we then do something different to address it?

It is my hope that these poems are a way for us to process the emotional effects of repeated gun violence. They are a space where the part of your heart aching over our current reality can come and know you are not alone.

Son of a Gun

is my son
the gun
or
is your son
the gun
or
if we load all mothers
do they become guns
or
did we all suck
the teats of guns
are we all
bright guns or bright bright suns
or
are you the gun

please can you tell me
is the gun
you

The Bullet Cures

The bullet asks to be the fire that melts it.

The bullet asks to be given back, returned to the earth. To become a bridge, a garden gate, a plant liner. A tent, enclosing instead of burying. A ring that keeps going and going, running from itself and into itself like wisdom, like love.

The bullet asks to be the cure. To turn into the helmet saving a head from crushing. To create the structured bones of a manmade waterfall. The bullet wants to be a shield. To be shingles on a roof. Provide cover. The bullet aches to serve a higher purpose. To be a wheelbarrow distributing seeds. To be the pin in your glasses, the tiny one that holds the whole thing together. To be as cold as an ice cream scoop, as warm as a pacemaker. To become what ticks in your watch.

The bullet asks to crumble in pieces. To be delicate like lace or a spiderweb. To transform into the jar or the candle it holds. To flicker and fade slowly, liquify as it's consumed. To live as an outdoor chair, abandoned. To die as one. Its rust the dirt reclaiming its victim.

The bullet wants to be the echo, not be echoed. The bullet wants to forget itself, to forget it was ever there.

The bullet asks to rest, to rest. To rest.

New Clothes

Once upon a time
there lived many emperors
looking up at so many
convocations of eagles
circling the sky it darkened.

In dimness the emperors exclaimed
look at my new wardrobe
individual hushed tones
thundering in everyone's ears
at once.

The many emperors preened
to no avail.
Eyes and ears
blocked
to truth or beauty.

With everything dark
and full of noise,
there was no way to tell
who wore what.
Survival became the game.

Hawks and vultures crowded
eagles in the sky.
One flew near a child
so close
its wings brushed his cheek.

Wind from its flight
opened up a piece of sky.

The child said:
The emperors have no clothes!
Another said:
No, look. I see them!
The finest gold and silver

threaded
with AR-15s
and AK-47s
and M16s
and shotguns.

Their barrels
are aimed outward.

Trigger Finger

itchy, you want to scratch
absentmindedly
with the butt of a gun
always available
locked and loaded

a part of our bodies now
a ghost made tangible
as much control
as our hands
for scratching itches

what itch
to scratch
that many
tiny hands
die for

finger bent and locked
limited movement
a finger bound
may straighten suddenly
with a snap

kill the still
innocent
because the rest of us
should know better
know each other better

the violence unwilling
to be stopped
thugs at all levels
of society
but dressed better

thugs know
celebrity politics is crowned
but precarious
thugs hold the armor
of your fear

to unravel you from you
lost to yourself
in the end
making everyone as empty
as you feel

fill people with their own fire
not bullets
not yours
watch fire glow and grow
and warm

Voices in the Field, I

"At the active shooting incident,
here's what happened—"

Active shooters are so rare.

"Yes, but, I was in one and—"

*Statistically, these situations
almost never happen.*

"Oh, but—"

*How about that game?
Did you see it?*

Unseeing

undulating in the breeze
like a sail

50 bullet holes instead of stars
red stripes bleeding

between white gauze strips
unable to contain

the wound
we cannot unsee

Light and Death

to follow the path of our own light
back to the sun
casting further and faster
than we can track

a lone star
a dimming flashlight
an eye glow
reflected in a screen

and thirteen counts
of lemons
both inside and outside
a basket

skipping digestion
turning directly into fading light
the prism bending
our right to be ourselves

an eye on the lantern
its trembling fire
our dented metal
can contain

not watching
the path ahead
but witnessing
how light jumps

how the dark creeps in
when there's a flash
then so much absence of light
we must all be blind now

sick of this other path
one psycho tread
and we don't need to go there
not turning away from the bodies exactly

but knowing where to spread light
where to find it
it's not in those halls
not down the barrel of that gun

if I could trace
the path of my own light
I'd know
where the burning is

I'd know how to forgive myself
for thinking
there's no light
among those bodies anymore

I'd know how to be the light
instead of the shattered lamp
searing because the bulb
is never coming back

the lamp has no place
for holding anymore
and light needs to be cradled
by our eyes

light needs to be set free
to glance off the water
like a bird launching from the tree
for the first time

Don't Say Gun

to the children
who will be next:
don't say gun.

to the adults
who will be next:
don't say male anger.

to all of us watching:
don't say prevention.

to the next shooter:
don't say tactical gear.

to the walls in the school:
don't say you see anything.

to the children
who are afraid to go to school:
don't say for the rest of your life.

to the father who says
homeschool is the answer:
don't say churches
malls
colleges
grocery stores
garlic festivals
synagogues
rallies
country music festivals
temples
streets
bars
mosques

hotel rooms
gas stations
night clubs
hospitals
parades
cars
bowling alleys
banks
post offices
neighborhoods
newsrooms
homes.

to the maps
turning redder every day:
don't say how town names
used to mean something
more than blood.

to the people who say
"it's godlessness in schools,"
as if the children deserve it:
say that evil, humans, and ideas
kill people.
but don't you dare say gun.

to everyone in America:
don't say what's invisible
might kill you.

Pull the Trigger

the call to action
even for a simple choice

straight to violence,
possible death

the choice unwinding from us
unwinds us

instead:
grab the rope swing

leap into water
step onto the dance floor

take an offered hand
push the door handle

breathe life into a balloon
pull the soul by its string

turn intention
into reality

by letting loose
a folding in the body

When Autocorrect Befriends Mad Libs

I need to make an appointment with my gun.
I need to make sure my fertility isn't gun. Let's
have some gun with friends. I drank too much
gun the other day and I'm finding it hard to
gun and bear it.

What do we have left to gun?

Praise be to gun.

Back to School Shopping List 2024

1. backpack (big enough to hide behind)
2. notebook (for reunification records)
3. textbooks (thick, so three in a row can stop a bullet)
4. a mini AR-15 (in kindergarten primary colors)
5. bulletproof vest, sizes 5T-Juniors XL (preferably if the market provides cute dresses or shirt and pant sets)
6. old clothes (for use as tourniquets)
7. spelling test (words: tourniquet, instructions, wound, direct, manual, pressure)
8. coffins (small)
9. vigil candles (many)
10. memorial flowers and favorite stuffed animals

The Bullet Never Quite Stops

The bullet asks to be the key.

The bullet asks to be round or spiral or a shape that travels up and down instead of one way. To be revered for what it can hold instead of what it takes away. The bullet asks to save itself. To run a marathon, for real: to keep running and running and never quite stop. To exist in the eyes and the ears instead of as a cold shadow to them.

The bullet longs to dissolve the distance between people and bring them closer, not further. Wants to smash walls and rip open locked things, to destroy what keeps us separate from each other. The bullet asks to turn rivers into ribbons. Wants to be the softness instead of what pierces it.

The bullet asks to turn around.

A Short Labor

she looked into holsters first
drawn by soft materials
American flag designs
exotic leathers

bags to carry
baby's necessities
and hide the gun
near diapers, pads, cream

they'd tried for years
to get a gun
seemed the bodies
were never quite ready

with many invasive procedures
much paperwork
and a lot
a lot of money

the constant questioning
of the working of the body
what it's capable
of harnessing

here they are on the big day
its slick metal shining
off her eyes
reflecting her smile in the gleam

waiting to be nursed
to fill with life
blood running from its parents
into the trigger and through the barrel

the happiest day of her life
lucky, a short labor
lucky, he's healthy
no birth defects

if there were
it's a matter of the clock
to tell us when
to disarm him

the heartbeat clicking of metal parts
too late to abort
the life that takes life
from those who give life

she holds him close
never wants to let go
birthing
lives with guns

Three Ways to Experience an Active Shooter Situation

After Rebekah Bloyd's "Three Views of a Woman Undergoing Treatment"

I. SOUND

Music, a sheet behind me.
Voices talking, laughing—
a layered blanket.
Children ahead of me
playing, squealing
on the fake grass.

My ears own the present,
register the pop pop—
two distinct sounds—
my body notes afterward
the precise time between
the shots,
not too short but not too long,
part of me recording it
even as the rest of my body
turns, laughs, carries forward
life and joy,
assuming those pop sounds
part of a Friday evening revelry.

I now know
the sound of gunshots in daylight.
They don't sound like much.
None of the long hollow echo
of the sound bleeding;
no serious finality expressed
from television.

I've been privileged—
my brain and body free most times
from dividing sounds into two buckets:
fatal and not.

When they release the Uvalde video,
a reporter writes:
"their screams have been edited out,"
something I didn't know
we should be thankful for.

II. TIME

The time between this shooting
right here right now
and the last shooting
tightens, contracts.

The play area drains
in less than five seconds.
I watch people run away
or fast walk
from the Apple store.
Urgency two-toned,
the glass-walled store emptying
in less than 10 seconds.

Part of my brain lost in time
considers ducking under the half wall,
musing about the lack of information—
don't want to get shot
cowering in that half-safe-space
pinned into victim.

The time between the shots
and when we act feels too long,
as we perk up like gazelles' ears
pointing to the sky, trying to glean
where the lion is, which direction
he comes, how long we'll have
to make a move.

We watch some people pause
their running, stop, look back, walk slowly
toward the direction they came.
Uncertainty crowding us—
we're stanchions—
the part where the wave dies out,
because it's unaware or too tired
or just no fun.

Time contracts, tightens,
bringing about a year ago
right back here, when another active shooter
was on the loose in the neighborhood,
us tightening the windows,
not sleeping at night,
clutching our children.

My first week in Austin
on a nighttime walk
two people pointed guns up a tree.
They waved them about
like second eyes, roving.

III. SPACE

Then the running.
I watch
all the parents scoop up
their children, a block of them
coming toward us,
panicked faces blurring.
Is it all their faces
or just one mother
my eyes zoom in on?

A crowd streaming toward us,
scattering after the intersection.

Two schools of fish
undecided about direction
but swirling anyway.
No plan—just chaos.

You know what would clear the air?
Another gun.

Are the people running from
collective trauma,
or running from Texas
and its gun laws
that capture freedom
and put it on a pedestal
to stare at those of us running past?

Space contracts.
Someone mentions another shooter,
another town, another Christmas.
The response: was that the one with
the backpack? The hats? The guidance counselor?
The parents that did. . . that did not?
Like teenagers, the names buried, lost
under surface salient features
as we struggle to distinguish
one violence from another.

Sound contracts. The body contracts,
bracing for impact,
the injury entering directly,
no chance of shield injuries
like seatbelts or airbag whiplash,
no anxiety from the moment of crash,
just a nest of people
enjoying life, then transforming
into a surging organism,
returning to the earth it forgot.

Assimilating Metal, the Heart Grasps

A man charges into a mall
with his hands pointed in front.
Marigolds fall from his fingers.

An active shooter enters a church.
All the guns in his arms
become snapdragons.

The person of interest near the playground
stumbles over the vines
suddenly winding around his body.

A suspicious person with intent
driving to the movie theater
has to stop to stare at the zinnias
flowing out the passenger window.

A person at their limit
decides to buy firearms,
but opens their hands
to accept buttercups and azaleas.

The bully's words shoot into the bullied,
whose body tries to assimilate metal,
only to find the heart grasps
violets and hyacinths.

#NotAllGuns

Not all guns kill people
but some do,
it's true.

The burden of proof
falling on the victims,
not the guns.

The gun is innocent
until proven
useful,

proven
they carry out
their intended task.

Until proven they exist
and only then can they
create harm.

A weapon that's a tool,
except always a weapon,
even in the woods.

Forget video games. Hunting's on.
A range is child's play.
What are the children thinking?

Not all men kill people,
it's true,
but some do.

Warning signs slipping
under freedom's guise
and new ways of not seeing each other.

Innocent
until proven
ferocious.

If a woman speaks up
against a man's abuse of power,
we hear:

#notallguns and #notallmen
but the weaponized and weaponizing
fear words as weapons.

Fear leads them to say
#allwomen
might do this.

Silenced and shamed
until proven
innocent.

I want to hear
from the guns
that don't shoot things.

Chekhov's Gun—or, the Second or Third Act

What Chekhov knew
was the heart of man.

The heart wants
what it wants,

and the movie's heart wants
an explosion.

The potential
must become actual

or we're all just in
a slow play

with no action. No plot.
Just characters

living life
with regular heartbeats.

How boring.
The details

of power
are not strenuous here

in the first act.
Unstrained.

We see people living
and settle into that net.

But instead of looking
at others or ourselves

let's look at the gun.
Wait for how the fire separates

those who do
from those that are done to.

Even games create divisions.
But entertainment must fire.

Under the Gun

I want to draw a comic
of all the things we let

lord over us
that isn't a lord

but the idea of a lord
pressing our heartbeats

pressuring our hearts
in 2023

until even good things feel
like we're waiting for the shot

the violence preparing
to unravel us

a breath held tight
to choke the living slowly

eat its life
more than death does

the dark, cold, wet
of ugly winter

is soothing
it's what's inside us

we counter by accepting
a warm fire

hot things
to eat or drink

savoring
how the couch and bed
hold us

Voices in the Field, II

"At the active shooting incident,
here's what happened—"

Want to hear about mine?

Hey, you should hear mine, too.

And mine.

Shapes

gun barrels have been stuck
in the same shape

for too many years
for one thing

they're too short
and look forward

too quick and convenient
to target

those in our way
to target a body

the barrel a black hole
an endless tunnel

an inside out knife
a portal to a worse dimension

the gun needs a second trigger
clicking on as gunpowder explodes

transforming the barrel
into a labyrinth

or a corn maze
that takes hours

or days
to exit

the second trigger
changing the barrel

to slope upward
like a reverse slide

only releasing bullets
to the sky

or sloping down
like Snuffleupagus's nose

though the earth and sky
have taken enough damage

how about a filigreed metal net inside
to catch the smoldering

before it goes anywhere?
or the ability to hold a person's anger

that's moving forward, toward us
see it, smell it, and hear it

and not let it into us
it's not my bullet, it's yours

Like Christmas

Jesus wants us
to celebrate his birth

by giving death
in a gun

to your son
assault style

it'll be the most
unforgettable gift

strangers will also receive
at a future day

turning into
a new dark holiday

give the green
teenager brain a gun

so he can paint
the town red

The Bullet Ages

The bullet asks to become a myth.

The bullet wants to be railroad tracks, to carry and guide a train's journey. To be the hammer and the nail but only in tables, chairs, bookshelves, cabinets—only things that hold up. Good secrets. You know the kind. The ones harboring love, not misery.

The bullet longs to be woven into a blanket. Or a rug. To be comforting, decorative. The bullet wants to age out of unreasonable expectations. Turn into wiring that connects. To not just send messages, but to listen to them.

The bullet would settle for being a TV. Or an antenna because the bullet's dying to be a receiver. The bullet dreams of living a life of obscurity as a clothes hanger where its body disintegrates in darkness over a million days.

The bullet asks to become a wheel. So going becomes the goal instead.

Sticking to Your Guns

your guns
glued to the body
the signs of violence
a living collage

our collected threats visible
the ways in which we're willing
to obliterate
now numbered for counting

how close to the surface our wounds
and our wound choices
how active
pressurized

how many volcanoes
bubbling
which hills lie between
the spillover and the towns in its path

when sticking to your guns
maybe you need stronger glue
to make them part of you
not us

when do you set them down
when do you let your body
live free
of carrying

The World We Live In

In 2023 a child runs
for her scooter
but finds a revolver.

Her brother reaches
for the markers,
which are rifles.

The blocks are handguns.
The dolls are shotguns.
The pencils are pistols.

I want a snack, she says.
But the crackers
are guns.

Even the tree
in the yard
is a firearm.

The bush
next to it
a machine gun.

Pretty soon
all words are guns.
This is how we communicate now.

Out of the Line of Sight

fewer snow days now / than shootings / drills / hard lockdowns / soft lockdowns / credible threats / non-credible threats / parent reunifications upon notice / texts and newsletters about ongoing situations / going from *it'll never happen here* / to the unsaid but enacted: / of course we know *the risk is higher now* / so get ready / the processes and words in place / as a defense / against / the indefensible / imminent threat / fortifying classrooms / we want our kids / to be innocent / but / we let their innocence be shot / asking them / to move away from windows / hide behind backpacks / turn invisible / become a ghost / so they can't be killed / or kill / shrink down so the evil overlooks them / looks past our culture of acceptable violence / looks past us / as we look past each other / we want to become out of sight / culpability a moving target

Voices in the Field, III

when mothers buy
their children phones

so in their last moments at school
at least they won't be alone

Notes Taken in Research for a Poem About School Shootings

After Elliot Harmon's "Notes Taken in Research for a Poem About *Ms. Pac-Man*"

School shootings are like car accidents:
women cause more fender-benders;
men cause fewer, but with more lethal harm.

No, wait, it's not like car accidents at all.

98% of mass shooters are male.
Looking at only gains, we deny losses.

Shootings are now silver fabric woven
in the quilt of attending school.

-

Uvalde is the only second I'm glad
Elliot isn't alive. He didn't need to see this.

-

The day after the Uvalde shooting
I banter at the grocery store with Albert.

He says to layer fish by their tails
when baking,

he learned from Julia and Jacques,
and we laugh at their drunkenness

or Frenchness that we share,
Albert being my grandfather's name.

I turn to leave; his face turns serious.
He nods. "Be safe out there."

I wander the dairy section,
the ghost of a shooter now entering behind me,
the ghost of myself, shrugging her shoulders.

-

I can't be safe.
What about my children?

What about the children?

-

N calls from California, shaken;
her heart drips imagining
the unimaginable with her son.

She wonders how I feel about my daughter
going to kindergarten this fall in Texas
less than an hour from Uvalde.

-

An NRA member says, "They need to stop
being such easy targets."

-

My in-laws ask about my daughter's school:
the teachers, the grades, the uniforms.

I say,
"No, what's most important
is how many doors it has."

\-

My physical therapist doesn't talk politics.
But she wants to say something here.
She wonders how many mass shooters are female.

Not many.
"Seems like a male problem," she says.

\-

Let's not get rid of war. Let's bring
the war to the youngest people.

\-

A girl I sat next to in English
sophomore year of high school
had a shot list.

We helped each other in class.
Had gone to a concert together.

I found out I was on her list.
On the first page. Top 10, in fact.

I asked her why.
She said she hated two of my friends,
they were fake assholes,
and she thought I'd want to die with them.

Even though by the time she wrote that list,
I wasn't friends with them.

To say this violence is senseless
is to ignore teenager reality.

-

My physical therapist didn't go watch
the fireworks this year, mostly

she was napping instead, but partly
it was the 4th of July shooting

at a parade in her hometown.
She wonders if anything

will change around guns
because this time
it's an affluent neighborhood.

-

One week after the Uvalde shooting
I call my mom in Massachusetts,

certain she'll mention the shooting this time,
say how worried she is about her grandchildren,

push me again to move
back there, from this latest atrocity.

Her silence is telling.
I ask her anyway.

She's casual
but her voice is already dead:
"No. It's everywhere now.
You can't get away from it."

Shoot It Down

can we let flight
take place

if the bird
is not for us

watch it disappear
fading

until the clouds
breathe it in

Texas 2022

Where it seems safer to have sex
with a gun
than a man.

Where it seems men
turn into guns—
forget the Freudian veil already.

Where it seems men
care only about spreading
bullets or blood.

bang!

the bullet leaves its chamber
moves backward with great force

picks up speed
past the bolt and firing pin

punctures the chest
of the shooter

misses the heart
exits in a clean hole

waits
buried in the wall
for someone to rescue it

the shooter's wound
now visible, bloody

life-threatening
a manifestation of festering

his child self
innocent and unscarred

rises up to hold
his man self

hugs him
as he bleeds

the bullet hole so big
light casts through it

collecting, sending out sharp
shards of light in glaring bits

like bullets
entering the hearts of all
who tender attention

Thicker Than Water

After H2O

slick hand in mine / she clings like the heat can suction her away / she feels its power omnipresent / pressing on our eyeballs / we don't want a savior / hazy distortion surrounding us / we can hardly see the school and its promises / we can barely surmise its warnings / we need more good guys and fewer guns / even in the glaze the day already heavy / all my possible failures float / insisting I catch them to control them / but some speed by / I sweat / is this the place where she'll die / fleeting but insistent / other possibilities freer / lightening air and one exhale / we don't need heroes / the teacher smiles at her / extends a hand / we don't want to need to be saved / just go about our day / the teacher reminds her to be calm / the learning passes between teachers and students / students and other students / friends / people now important to each other / interwoven / leave us alone / carrying each other moment to moment / remembering smiles as scaffolds / people as ledges in the cliff climb / trading sweetness / it's time we count them / even if the possibility / is not enough to save

The Bullet Renames

The bullet asks to be a pipe that holds water. A conduit. To eat its own energy.

The bullet longs to abandon itself mid-flight and become weighted at the bottom of the sea, holding a boat aloft.

The bullet asks to be the sound of buttons falling to the floor. The sound of feathers resettling in a pillow. To be a holy sound instead of its opposite. To be renamed into and then out of its terror. To be as large and powerful and revered as the sun; which is to say, to have the basic grace to be useful and taken for granted.

The bullet wants to give out delicate shades of light, passing over no one with this glory. The bullet asks to be a divining rod, a rake, or a crucifix.

The bullet asks to be a space rather than creating one.

The Sun Beams Down

dandelions flee
daisies shelter in place
roses staunch the bleeding

in chaos
no one can see
which bulbs
are coming or going

pansies evacuate
gathering in the road
irises await
footage from the scene

lilies remain on lockdown
lavender rushes
to the reunification site

sorting out victim stems
from survivor leaves

magnolias visit the makeshift memorial
tulips tell us about trauma

carrion flowers offer thoughts and prayers
say: don't make this political

when the sun beams down
on the flowers
begin the cycle again

Shooting Blanks

the male process
of giving life

is compared
with a weapon of death

and to wound
without killing

is weak
and discarded

what if the gun
was blank instead?

clear
an insubstantial wisp

barely in the hand
fading into the sunset

a container
we can't open

its face of glass
reflecting the owner's eyes

a mirror—
reputed to steal souls—

this mist-like gun
returned your soul to you instead

not simply a vessel
accepting force

(if that's how you think
of sex, I'm sorry)

things and people
are carriers

we become less simple
than the outlines

of gun, victim, perpetrator
set against
parent, lover, child

Stone, Not Seed

moving toward the corner
where the shots were fired

part of me still wants
to run away

every time
a stone in my belly

each moment noting
this hesitation, still marked

like the daughter
whose father was shot at a bar

how she feels
when she hears the word gun

how the active shooter drill
traumatized the front desk personnel

so many people now directly or indirectly
touched by gun violence

the choice
to pick up more guns

or run
into this sick stomach feeling

something unseen
but no less dangerous

stones cast as another weapon
piled on a door

a weight to sink in the water
to sit atop a grave

or to fold in the waves
eroding its sharpness

revealing the beauty immovable
or set in a design around a tender sprout

Triggered

to be triggered is to be a trigger
to someone else's triggering

you're triggered
meaning you're having a reaction

feeling angry or sad
or something you don't want to feel

someone telling you
you're triggered

instead of
I'm sorry

is fingering another trigger
aimed at your face

and you feel
the harm

because guns are all around
like flies in sunshine

even the language we use
to protect each other

to honor humanity
is loaded

There Are No Answers in Children's Stories

the anime trees wave in the breeze
                metal, always metal
the horses chuff
                often dark
letting us know whether they're happy
                coming with an embedded shadow
or unhappy
                in an aimed hand
in the forest
                a line toward the target
this animated breath
                a sleek danger
the fox biting out of fear
                running out its anger
anime characters turn into
                holding the hand
the cat, the dog, and the rat
                that shoots it hostage
with a hug
                cold metal, too hard
the ohmu's red red eyes
                unyielding
see parents turn into pigs
                there's no surprise here
the dragon river spirits
                a bullet from a gun invisible
laughing in the sky
                a story with one ending
free at last
                a one-way ticket
telling us stories of consumption
                no matter how many bullets
against nature
                the end result is death

the yak who brings us to healing waters
                    selves obliterated
the boars and wolves and chimps
                    can magnify
taking on the violence adults spread

Voices in the Field, IV

in Survival Strategies 101,
teachers counsel kids to

run as fast as you can
in many different directions

and we wonder
why they don't test well

The Bullet Gives Away

The bullet asks to be a continued dream, a mere figment of your imagination. To be a gift.

The bullet wishes to be a prosthetic hand or an umbrella. To prop up the hospital bed, asking nothing of others. The bullet wants to be a buckle or a bucket, to hold itself up and to fill itself. To mutate into a music stand or perhaps a whistle. To draw worlds of shapes as a half-used pencil.

The bullet asks to be a near-miss, a lost love, a never-has-been. A camera. To see the stranger you can turn your back on. To measure the tides of the sea. To magnetize itself to itself.

The bullet longs to be a question mark. To dissolve like an ice cube and ignore its own boundaries. To be less decisive.

The bullet asks for a halo and angel wings, but only so it can give them away.

Riding Shotgun

like it's a horse
or a nuclear bomb

the goal of first,
upfront, special

don't want to miss
the front seat of destruction

see the collision up close
float on the moment

before impact
wrought on each other

passing trauma back and forth
like a hot potato

a winner in the front
loser sulking in the back

the backseat
an opportunity to rest

to know oneself
and feel how to survive here

what arms we take up
to survive others' chaos

NO, I refuse to consume that
to let my system be destroyed

by your poison
by your bullets

my gun is NO
and it stops here

AUTHOR'S NOTES

The five bullet poems in this collection were inspired by K-Ming Chang's novel *Bestiary*, specifically her line: "a bullet doesn't ask to be given back." All five of the poems would not exist without K-Ming Chang's line, but it is not credited on each poem because it was noted on the first one and then separately again here.

"Don't Say Gun"—the listing of places where gun violence has taken place is intended to be a moment of silence for each of these major events that are now household names:

churches: Charleston, South Carolina (2015) 9 killed, 1 injured
malls: Allen, Texas (2023) 8 killed, 7 injured
colleges: Blacksburg, Virginia (2007) 32 killed, 23 injured
grocery stores: Buffalo, New York (2022) 10 killed, 3 injured
garlic festivals: Gilroy, California (2019) 3 killed, 17 injured
synagogues: Pittsburgh, Pennsylvania (2018) 11 killed, 6 injured
rallies: Tucson, Arizona (2011) 6 killed, 13 injured
country music festivals: Las Vegas, Nevada 60 killed, 413 injured
temples: Oak Creek, Wisconsin (2012) 6 killed, 4 injured
streets: too many to list
bars: Thousand Oaks, California (2018) 13 killed, 17 injured
mosques: Christchurch, New Zealand (2019) 51 killed, 40 injured
hotel rooms: Las Vegas, Nevada (2022) 3 killed
gas stations: Columbus, Georgia (2023) 9 injured
night clubs: Orlando, Florida (2016) 49 killed, 53 injured
hospitals: Tulsa, Oklahoma (2022) 4 killed, unspecified others injured
parades: Chicago, Illinois (2022) 7 killed, 48 injured
cars: Farmington, New Mexico (2023) 3 killed, 6 injured
bowling alleys: Lewiston, Maine (2023) 18 killed, 13 injured
banks: Louisville, Kentucky (2023) 5 killed, 8 injured
post offices: Edmond, Oklahoma (1986) 14 killed, 6 injured
neighborhoods: Cleveland, Texas (2023) 5 killed

newsrooms: Annapolis, Maryland (2018) 5 killed, 2 injured

homes: too many to list

These aren't the only churches, malls, colleges, etc. where mass shootings have taken place. These are some of the most notable ones. What's absent from this list (but echoes behind all these) are the school shootings.

"Like Christmas"—in at least three of the school shooting cases, we hear the parents, upon hearing of warning signs in their teenagers, gave them guns for Christmas instead of following the recommendations of professionals. In one of the cases, the teen Brenda Spencer stated her father "bought the rifle so I would kill myself."

"The World We Live in"—hearing about particular shootings gives me the impression the shooter has no other way to communicate. We have not been listening or seeing them for a long time. The Covenant School, Nashville, Tennessee (2023) 3 killed, 3 injured.

"Notes Taken in Research for a Poem About School Shootings"—The fact that 98% of mass shootings have male perpetrators is something we need to look at further. There's something more here than guns, and what can we then do about it? I have found sources that cite the number as 97%, 94%, etc. From one source: "…it seems wrong to blame mass killings in particular on toxic masculinity. That's because male rage can be deadly at any time or any place, and at every level of analysis."

https://slate.com/news-and-politics/2017/10/what-the-white-mass-shooter-myth-gets-right-and-wrong-about-killers-demographics.html.

I don't intend to lump all males together in this horrific category. But we need to look deeper—it's not just about guns. What are we missing about anger, specifically? At the time of Uvalde, these were the things being said to me and were in that atmosphere. The only almost-mass shooter I personally know is female (which is already in that poem). The NRA member quote "They need to stop being such easy targets" echoes what Brenda Spencer, the school shooter at Grover Cleveland Elementary School, told police negotiators: "the children and adults were easy targets." San Diego, California (1979) 2 killed, 9 injured.

"Texas 2022"—In 2021, Texas passed House Bill 918, which lowered the age from 21 to 18 to be eligible for a license to carry a handgun. https://capitol.texas.gov/BillLookup/History.aspx?LegSess=87R&-Bill=HB918

They also passed House Bill 1927, which allows Texans to carry handguns in public without a license and the background check and training that a license requires. https://capitol.texas.gov/BillLookup/History.aspx?LegSess=87R&-Bill=HB1927

Texas also passed Senate Bill 8, which prohibits abortions as early as six weeks into pregnancy, "when a heartbeat is detected by ultrasound." Embryos at this developmental stage don't possess a heart. Medical and legal experts say the sound Republican lawmakers are referring to is the motion of electrical pulses stimulating muscle cells in a tube that will eventually become part of the heart. As part of this prohibition, in lieu of government enforcement, private individuals can sue abortion providers or people who assist abortion, enabling neighbors to become vigilantes. https://capitol.texas.gov/BillLookup/History.aspx?LegSess=87R&-Bill=SB8

Nine months after these bills went into effect, and a day after his birthday, an 18-year-old legally purchased weapons and used them at the Robb Elementary School shooting in Uvalde, Texas, May 24, 2022. This happened 10 days after the May 14, 2022 Buffalo, New York shooting, and before the

2022 4th of July shooting at a parade in Highland Park, Illinois. The Supreme Court officially overturned Roe v. Wade in June 2022. https://www.npr.org/2022/06/24/1102305878/supreme-court-abortion-roe-v-wade-decision-overturn

"Thicker Than Water"—On the first day of kindergarten, my daughter was scared. A bright, friendly teacher welcomed her in and was the first voice, face, and hand to connect to my child, making her feel comfortable at the new school. Mrs. Ara Duke continued to be amazing each day: kind, smart, cheerful. A brilliant soul. I knew her daily as a fabulous person—someone this broken world needed. She was an innocent bystander at a local celebratory concert. As Prophetess Cynthia Nunn said at Ara Duke's memorial service: "Her life is still speaking. And oh, what a life it was." Round Rock, Texas (2024) 2 killed, unspecified others injured.

Mrs. Ara Duke's passion for education and bettering the lives of children everywhere led her to attend NPH events and volunteer. To celebrate her life, a portion of the proceeds of this book will be donated in her name to NPH. https://nphusa.org/ara/

"The Sun Beams Down"—the language occurring at each of these incidents in the news piles up over time and is a script now.

"There Are No Answers in Children's Stories"—animal descriptions are from animated movies, mostly from Hayao Miyazaki's films. These animals are usually sidekicks, friends, and familiars. *Nausicaa, Fruits Basket, Spirited Away, Princess Mononoke*

ACKNOWLEDGMENTS AND GRATITUDE

I am grateful to the following organizations for recognizing and publishing poems from this collection.

- "The Bullet Cures," "The Bullet Never Quite Stops," and "The Bullet Gives Away," *Ephemera Literary's* July 2023 poet of the month.
- "The Bullet Cures" won the 2023 Poetry Super Highway Contest.
- "The Bullet Renames" won the 2024 Plaza Prose Poetry Contest.
- "Son of a Gun" *Poetry Super Highway,* and nominated for a Pushcart prize.
- "The Bullet Cures" *Sappho's Torque.*
- "The Bullet Ages" was chosen as a finalist in the ESWA Crossroads 2024 contest.
- "Notes Taken in Research for a Poem About School Shootings" first appeared on the radio show Poetry Bread Presents, hosted by T.A. Niles.

When I look back at the creation of this book, I'm amazed at the amount of help it has received to come into the world, more than anything I've written yet. I've heard tales of (and have also experienced) people coming out of the woodwork to tell a writer not to pursue a particular project. But this one? The opposite.

People's words and help nudged it back on the rails many times.

At every turn, I've received more community support than I thought possible. Sharing some of these poems in public immediately received strong reactions. People needed this. If I, in my little corner over here, am having these feelings about this issue, then why is it ridiculous to think others may be feeling this as well? They're living in it and through it, too. Even when it was not about the words, people kept coalescing around me to offer support on literary contracts, cover concepts, and discussions around gun violence. This project has truly been for the people and with the people.

I hope I have half the courage of writers who have inspired me with their truth-telling. Thank you to Claudia Rankine for *Citizen*, Patricia Smith for *Incendiary Art*, Traci Kato-Kiriyama for *Navigating Without Instruments*, Joaquín Zihuatanayo for *Occupying Whiteness*, and Stalina Emmanuelle Villarreal for *Watcha*. Thank you to Ani Difranco for being one of the first truth-teller artists I encountered, and for all her music over the years. I have been able to stand up and say these words because of their daring.

Thank you to many people for lending me their words, their hugs, their own boldness. To the late Judith Serin, I treasured our friendship, and I am also grateful she took time and effort to provide exacting yet supportive feedback on my work—especially this manuscript.

Thank you to Michael G. Hickey for helping me see what's good about having a bunch of shooting/gun poems together after all. Also, thanks, Michael, for continuing to check in about the status of the manuscript, providing enthusiasm and emotional support at key moments. Thank you, T.A. Niles, for often championing my work and for your friendship, along with also making specific suggestions and kind comments for these poems.

Thank you to Rick Lupert of the Cobalt Cafe and Poetry Super Highway. You do so much to help poets and poetry that it's hard to put it all into words. Thank you to the judges of the Poetry Super Highway 2023 Contest—Kathrynn Axton, Ashley Cline, and Jan Harris—for choosing "The Bullet Cures" as the winning poem.

To all the Cobalt poets, thank you for sharing community, your talents, and your courage for being your true selves.

Thank you to the Plaza Prizes and to Simon Kerr. Thank you to the judge of the Plaza Prose Poetry 2024 Contest—Carrie Etter—for choosing "The Bullet Renames" as the winning poem.

Thank you to the Eastern Shore Writers Association and the judge, Nancy Mitchell, for choosing "The Bullet Ages" as a top 10 finalist in the Crossroads 2024 Contest.

Thank you, Syr Beker and Britta Jensen, specifically, for your moral support around a gnarly literary industry issue that included some of these poems. You gave me virtual hugs when I needed them most.

Thank you to Syr, Hollie Hardy, Stalina, Krishna Asundi, and Paul Corman Roberts for giving me guidance around writing contracts for that same industry issue.

Syr, thank you also for adding your voice to the support of what a group of gun poems had to offer (and for general writing support, community, friendship, and your brilliant writing). And then, of course, thank you for literary auntie information, encouragement, support, and pushes. You were so patient in coaching me not to self-reject and submit to dream publishers.

To Amanda Chiado, Jessica Wickens, Amanda Mamykon, Allison Goldstein, Stalina, and Hollie—thank you for general writing support, community, and close friendship. You're fantastic writers and people who continue to raise the bar.

Thank you to Nithya Krishnan and Farzane Takbiri. You are always excited about my writing, even when no one else is. You're such a light, besides being intelligent and there for me when I need it with other life stuff.

A big thank you and hugs to my Writers' League of Texas women: Roanna Flowers, Kara Stockinger, and Annie Williams, who championed one of these poems and seconded support for a group of poems with shooting/guns all together. You're so funny and smart and such a joy to be around. I'm lucky to know y'all. Roanna, that's the best use of ma'am I've ever heard. Thank you.

Lacey Wood, I appreciate your friendship and solidarity. You've given me beautiful responses that I hold close to my heart, including about one of these poems. Thank you.

Thank you to my late friend Elliot Harmon, whose fabulous poem I tried to model one of these poems after. Thank you to Kat—I'm sorry I wrote what I wrote without warning, but I'm grateful you understand what I meant. Thanks for letting me "steal" his work.

Tawan Udtamadilok, not only is your multifaceted and multitalented way of being a huge inspiration to me, but I'm so grateful we could laugh and cry together on a regular basis, and that we shared this artistic journey for a long time. To my partner in Creator's Life crime!

Thank you Savita and Daniel. These poems are borne out of my fierce love for you, and my broken heart that you have to worry about how "my new school doesn't have a ledge we can hide under. Now a bad man outside can see right into where we are." And that, at age 7, Savi, you now know the tragedy of losing the first teacher to welcome you into school.

Krishna, thank you for your daily partnership and ability to ride the storms of 2023 together (and also 2017 to now). It means the world to me.

Raquelle Lawrence, thanks for enhancing my children's lives, taking care of them, and also riding the storms of 2021-2024 with us. I appreciate your wise perspective. I hope that our multifaceted, deeper conversations around guns and gender come across in these poems.

Thank you to Kate Mobley for saying my manuscript was stunning and providing encouragement to submit to Mouthfeel Press. A massive thank you to Maria Miranda Maloney for publishing this book! When you said my manuscript moved you to the core as a mother, citizen, and publisher, I knew it found the right home. A writer can hear no better words. Thank you also for your excellent editing, keen eye, and openness to discussions. Thank you to everyone I worked with at Mouthfeel Press, for your efforts and dedication. A special thank you to Enzo Rodríquez Suárez, who designed a cover that's compelling, emotional, and empathetic, holding so much of what I hope this book does for readers.

Thank you, Syr, for the motorcycle jacket for my heart.

Thank you, Hollie, for reminding me it's not that big of a deal.

Thank you to those who gave me cover tips, advice, ideas, and sketches: Krishna, Allison, Miah Jeffra, Sarah Rosenthal, Britta, Lacey, Kara, Nithya, Roanna, Judith, Nancy Knight, Syr, Rick, and Paul.

Thank you, Jeffrey Bryant and Susan Calvillo, for reading a version and providing helpful commentary. Jeffrey, thanks for seeing this work's multitudes, and Susan, thanks for the concise, actionable feedback.

Thank you, Judith, for your words during another freakout. This book needed much emotional support.

Thank you to S.C. Says, Joaquín, Hollie, Jeffrey, and Stalina for your kind and thoughtful words about this manuscript. I appreciate how you took time out of your busy and amazing lives to consider this book.

Thank you to Winter Clark for all your help over the years, but especially when we found out together that my daughter's teacher had died. Thank you to all those who supported me emotionally during that time—you know who you are. Thank you Carrie Kaufman for your nuanced parenting counsel. Thank you, Rebekah Bloyd, for reminding me that people who really see you have a protective effect.

A book does not come about just because I wrote it—it arises from others' belief, support, and efforts to turn it into this tangible thing we hold. For each of the people named here, I believe this book would not exist without you. Thank you for adding your magic along the way. If you're reading this, you're someone who, even if you didn't directly support this book or these poems (well you did by buying it!) you have likely already supported me in other writing projects, with general love and kindness for me, or just by being the best you can be, and I'm happy to know you. Your magic rubs off even if you don't think so.

ABOUT THE AUTHOR

Heidi Kasa writes poetry and fiction. She received the 2024 Plaza Prose Poetry Prize and the 2023 Poetry Super Highway Prize for poems from *The Bullet Takes Forever*. She is also the author of *The Beginners*, winner of the 2023 Digging Press Chapbook contest, and *Split* (Monday Night Press, 2022). Kasa's writing has appeared in *Barrelhouse*, *The Pinch Journal Online*, and *The Brooklyn Rail*, among others. When she's not working as an editor, she's making artist books and necklaces in Austin.

Find her at www.heidikasa.com.